November 11, 2019

Dear Timmy,
Your Papa loves you and hopes you enjoys this book.

Yaro the Super Sleuth

In the Case of the Mystery Letter

A Top Secret Case Study of Grown-ups
<u>THIS</u> <u>BOOK</u> <u>IS</u> <u>ABOUT</u> <u>GROWN-UPS</u>
<u>FOR</u> <u>CHILDREN'S</u> <u>EYES</u> <u>ONLY</u>!!

Helen L. Edwards

By Helen L. Edwards

Illustrations by Chi Lam Chan

Yaro the Super Sleuth
in the Case of the Mystery Letter

Copyright 2009 by Helen L. Edwards

All rights reserved.

No part of this publication may be reproduced, or stored in a retrieval system, or transmitted in any form by any means, electronic, mechanical, photocopying, recording, or otherwise without written permission from the publisher. For information regarding permission, please write to: Permissions Department, Brain Candy Publishing, P.O. Box 198126, Des Moines, Washington 98198.

Text copyright 2009 by Helen L. Edwards
Illustrations by Chi Lam Chan

Colorist, Front and Back Cover Designer, Al Doggett
Copy editors, Esther Ervin and Elizabeth LaBelle
Book Design and Layout by Esther Ervin Fine Art, Seattle, Washington

Ages 9 and up

ISBN 13 978-0-9765414-0-0
ISBN 10 0-9765414-0-8

Contents

4. Dedication
5. Acknowledgements
6. The Story: Yaro the Super Sleuth in the Case of the Mystery Letter
46. Appendix A. Name Origins
46. Appendix B. Self-Discovery
48. Appendix C. Dr. Howard Gardner's Multiple Intelligences
49. Appendix D. Goal Setting
50. Appendix E. The Blueprint
51. Appendix F. Character: Who You Really Are
53. Appendix G. The Power Of Faith And Belief
53. Appendix H. Making It Happen In Your School
54. Career Awareness Exploration
54. Appendix I. Parents' Role
55. About the Author
55. About the Illustrator
55. About the Colorist

DEDICATION

This book is dedicated to my nephew Delvon K. Wilson, who is and always has been an inspiration to our family; and to my niece Nilesha K. Davis, who is the joy of my life. I will be proud of her Cum Laude college graduation forever.

TO ALL OF MY SIBLINGS: I Thank God for our family. I love each and every one of you. We are a family unit and each of you have helped me grow as a person. We will always remember the contributions to our family of our two siblings no longer with us, Vetress Bon Edwards, Jr., and Arlene Edwards. We know love never dies. I offer my heart-felt thanks to Bonnie Jean Edwards-Wilson, Aquibalon Zaki Ruquiya, Joan Marie Edwards, and Darryl Curtis Edwards.

ACKNOWLEDGEMENTS

I would like to acknowledge family and friends who have blessed my life in so many ways: Chekesha Davis, Jovon Stowers, Leondray Stowers, Leilani Kawaii Jones, Christopher Wilson, Iman Wilson, Umoya McKinney,Shavon Walworth, David Walworth, Lisa Pooser Wilson, Diallo Wilson, Zuberi Wilson, Kwalik Wilson, Vonda Edwards Hyman, Racine Edwards Silva, M.D., Delores Washington, Daniel Auberry, Tony Rose, Yvonne Rose, Lawrence R. Mason, Teri Woods, Michelle K. Jones, Sharone Valbush, Evelyn Brewster, Chantal Garza, Scott, Kelly Carroll, Christopher M. Williams, Dr. Elaine Love James, Jessie Matthews Spencer, Cindy Miller, Patricia Pawlikowski, Mary Schroeder, Chuck Tuman, Susan Theckston, Robin Lamoureux, Georgia Gwyn, Karen Chappon, Camisa Malmanger, Juanita Bell, Dennis Storkson, Wardell D. Patterson, Roger Evans, Kenneth Ames, Donna Ames, Kendra Ames, Delma Dawkins, Valerie Carter, Judith Bennett, Rebecca Sahm, Karen Carter, Katherine Greenberg, Tina Hause, Sandra Klein, Harriett Collins, Dorothy Swent, Teniea Sandlin, Debbi Needham, Ann Stewart, Margery Sisson, Celeste Borowiak, Kimberlee Goodman, Jennifer Rios, Jaqueline Shin, Scot Robertson, Alecia Rochelle, Helen Jacobson, Christie Brown, Paula McClurg, Sandra Rabago, Elizabeth Andaluz, Susan Hislop, JoAnne Williams, Sheri Swanson, Wendy Curtis, Jamie Soule, Jo Ellen McGrath, Cindy Busler, Hannah Woodall, Roy Hammock, Michael Grife, Drena Sabbatini, Rebecca Williams, Summer Yost, Jeanette Yee, Steve Saville, Janice Brandt, Erica Gregory, Cindy Wilkins, Deborah Gardner, Mona Bilgren, Roberta Reardon, Diane Evans, Barbara Vail, Evelyn Brewster, Andrea Matthews Rogers, Kay Matthews Johnson, Berni Fryrear, Sandy Smith, Lutricia A. Thompson, Diane Lynn Carper, Pamela Witkowski, Alison Dostert, Dave Larsen, Boyd Collins, Jacquelyn Hill, Shelia Palfrey, Frieda Takamura, Paige Foy, Ben Ibale, Eula McMillian Jones,Glendora Eaglin, Rosa Cook, Angelita Pizarro, Yvonne Miller, Anegbeode Mohammed, Dominic Corr, Francisco Martinez, Francisco Segura, Jocelyn Merhab, Ann Stewart, Mary Prichard, Rosa Cook, and Chase Michaelson.

Hi friends, my name is Yaro. My dad named me. Yaro means "son." I would like to introduce my trusty sidekick to you, "Saidi" my dog. I named him. His name means "helper." Saidi was trained at the Top Dog Obedience School. My dad said this school ranks among the best obedience dog schools in our nation. You see, Saidi is no dumb dog. He is quite smart and graduated at the top of his class.

Sometimes, when Saidi does the occasional "bad dog thing" my dad complains about all the money he spent sending Saidi to obedience school. Like the time dad had to take a business call, and he left his hamburger on the kitchen counter. When dad returned to find his hamburger missing, Saidi was licking up the last crumbs. Dad went straight for the newspaper. Saidi ran out of the back door. He spent the rest of the evening staying out of my dad's sight and hiding in his doghouse.
Have you ever watched the things grown-ups do? Or listened to what they say? I have, and sometimes it makes me wonder about them.

****WARNING****WARNING****WARNING****WARNING****
STOP!!! TOP SECRET CASE STUDY

If you are a grown-up, please do not read any further without asking a kid's permission. Thank you for cooperating!

I am going to be a detective when I grow-up. Saidi is going to be my partner. First, we need experience. Detectives spend a lot of time observing and asking questions.

"Saidi, sit! You graduated from Top Dog Obedience School, at the head of your class. I now deputize you. Saidi, you are now my official deputy dog! As good detectives, our relatives will never even know they are under surveillance. Saidi, we must keep good records and write down our observations. Our first case study is 'Eyes and Ears on Grown-ups in Action.' Come on Saidi, you can watch, sniff, and listen."

"Hold up!" I stopped in my tracks.
It's Missy Ann; I am not a fan. That girl is full of drama!

"Spying on me again, Missy Ann!"

"Don't flatter yourself. I just happened to be in my own backyard when I saw the spectacle of you deputizing Saidi through the bushes," she said as she handed me a torn, taped, and tattered letter. "I have a decoding job for you."

"Where did you get this letter?" I asked.
"I got it from my brother Shaquan's waste basket," Missy Ann replied.
"I don't know about this, Missy Ann. Technically, this letter is Shaquan's property."
Miffed, Missy Ann countered, "No, it is not! Once he threw it away, it became mine."

I was puzzled looking at the pages of numbers. I thought: *"How can I decipher this secret code?"*

With a sting in her voice Missy Ann snarled, "Yaro, if you don't have the confidence to crack the code to this 'Mystery Letter,' I will just tell the whole school you are no Sherlock Holmes."

I thought to myself: *This girl can ruin a reputation. She makes it her business to know everybody else's business, and then she tells it. Missy Ann doubted my skills. I had to prove myself.*

"I'm in the business of solving mysteries," I said. In my mind, I almost felt like a traitor to her older brothers, Shaquan and Kwame. They always have our backs in the neighborhood. They let us younger guys play ball with them and even give us tips. I felt uneasy taking on Missy Ann's case.

Then I remembered that my dad says, *"In America, everyone deserves representation."* That included Missy Ann.

"Missy Ann, you are not my only case," I said. "Do not call me or come see me. I will let you know when I have cracked the code."

"Yeah, yeah," said Missy Ann as she walked back to her house. "Just get the job done, and don't take forever."

"Saidi, the sign of a true professional is to stay focused and not get side-tracked. We will take this letter to my bedroom, date it for today, April 1, and put it in a private place. I just hope Missy Ann's case is not an April Fool's joke!"

As I left my bedroom, I heard loud voices and laughter.

"Look Saidi, there are our relatives making a big fuss over the baby!" I instantly felt sick! For a few seconds, no one even noticed me.

Then Auntie said, "Yaro baby, you are growing up and getting so tall and handsome."

Grandma chimed in, "Yes, he is, and he is smart and well mannered too." I started to feel good, and I stood tall with my chest sticking out.

Mom said, "Yaro helps me with the baby. He is an excellent big brother."

I just stood there and smiled my biggest smile. Having an adorable baby sister in the family is a big adjustment. But I am learning to live with it.

The case of "Eyes and Ears on Grown-Ups in Action"

April 1st

Well, Saidi, we had a full day. What did we note about grown-ups? They are fascinated by babies, who can do absolutely nothing!

STRANGE!!! Yaro &

Today, I went to church with Grandma. We sat next to Jamal and his parents. Mother Jordon was talking back to the preacher, as usual, saying things like, "Preach!" "Amen!" "Tell it!" "Tell the truth!"
Sister Dupree was crying, flapping her arms, and running up and down the church aisles shouting "Hallelujah!" She was accompanied by two ushers fanning her and keeping her from running into the pews. All this used to scare me, but Grandma told me that these sisters are really happy. That is just how they express themselves when the spirit moves them.

At home, Dad was watching the game with my uncle and grandpa.

The women were all in the kitchen preparing Sunday dinner.

The case of "Eyes and Ears on Grown-Ups in Action"
April 2nd

In church grown-ups can talk out loud, interrupt the preacher, shout, and run up and down the aisles, all because they are happy and the spirit moves them. Somehow, I think if kids did the same thing, we would be in big trouble. Something to ponder. . .
                                                            Yaro &

The next day at school, I managed to avoid Missy Ann all day.

After school my luck ran out when I heard a familiar voice shout, "Sherlock!" Yes, Missy Ann had spotted me! "Yaro, you know I am calling you out!" Missy Ann said as she stood there on the sidewalk surrounded by her girlfriends. I felt like a mouse caught in a trap.

"So what's up with the case of my Mystery Letter?"
I felt a half dozen eyes staring at me. I spoke in my most convincing voice under the circumstances.
"Missy Ann, I told you I had other cases."

Missy Ann roared with the confidence of a lion, "Yaro, I am not your average client! I am a VIP! In case you didn't know, 'Sherlock,' that means a Very Important Person! They don't call me 'The Mouth' for nothing. You get busy on my case pronto!"

I just stood there speechless and stepped aside as she and the girls passed by. Man, I could have kicked myself. Why did I just stand there like that? I could tell Missy Ann was going to be the client from "Badgerville!"

At home, Dad checked my homework. I aced it! Afterwards, I took out the garbage and played with Saidi in the yard. Saidi leaped, caught the ball in mid air every time, and didn't miss once. He was fearless.

A flash of fear washed over me as I thought back to my run-in at school with Missy Ann and her girlfriends. *I wonder if I can crack the code to that Mystery Letter.* I have never cracked a code before. I knew she was right, I did lack confidence.

I had to talk to my dad. I headed straight to my dad's office. He was busy at his computer.

I asked, "Dad, are you busy?"

"When you see me in my office, I am always busy," he said. "But I am never too busy for you. What's going on?"

"I have a problem," I said.
"I'm listening." He turned away from his computer to face me.

Slowly, I began, "I am afraid I might fail at something I have never tried before and everybody will find out."

Dad replied, "Everyone has failed at something. There is no shame in failing. There is shame in never trying, or in giving up. Use fear as a tool, as a warning in cases of danger, or as a motivator in competition; but never as an excuse for failing to try. You build confidence by giving something your best shot, with a 'can do' attitude."

We gave each other the "brother handshake" and a hug. I left Dad's office feeling pumped up and confident.

I went into the kitchen for a glass of juice. Mom was bottling milk for my sister.

I said, "Mom, have you ever been afraid to do something?"

"Let me think about that for a moment," she said. As I walked over to the refrigerator, she said, "Yes, I was afraid to become your mother."

I was not expecting such an odd response. It sounded crazy to me, and it seemed like I said, "What?!" and "Why?!" all at the same time.

My mother continued, "You are my first born. I wanted to be a good mom to you."

Now, it didn't sound crazy to me. I said, "Oh, Mom, you are the best mom on the planet!"

"Yaro," she said, "I love being your mom. Once I laid eyes on you, joy replaced my fears." She continued, "You made it easy, and when I had your sister, I knew I could do it. The fear was gone." I gave my mom the biggest hug.

Entering my bedroom with Saidi, I started telling myself I had a "can do" attitude as I pulled the torn, taped, and tattered letter out of my desk drawer. I scanned it for clues.

The first thing I noticed is that there were two sets of Roman numerals going from I to VII. It wasn't clear to me if it was a list ranking something in order of importance, or if it was just a list of items or names. It was clear to me this letter had been written cryptically to hide something. There was punctuation in the letter, which meant it could be read if translated properly. The key to cracking the code was to convert the numbers into letters! I figured that the numbers represented letters.

Code

A	1	Z
B	2	Y
C	3	X
D	4	W
E	5	V
F	6	U
G	7	T
H	8	S
I	9	R
J	10	Q
K	11	P
L	12	O
M	13	N
N	14	M
O	15	L
P	16	K
Q	17	J
R	18	I
S	19	H
T	20	G
U	21	F
V	22	E
W	23	D
X	24	C
Y	25	B
Z	26	A

X	O	F	Y
24	15	6	25
C	L	U	B

24 15 6 25   19 12 6 8 22   24 19 22   24 16 15 18 8 7
8 19 26   10 6 26 13   25 9 18 13 20   7 19 22
15 18 8 7   12 21   18 7 22 14 8   6 13 23 22 9
2 12 6   9   13 26 14 22.   14 22 22 7   6 8
26 7   7 19 22   24 15 6 25   19 12 6 8 22   7 19 22
8 26 14   23 26   2   26 13 23   7 18 14 22
4 22   23 18 8 24 6 8 8 22 23 26 7   12 6 9
15 26 8 7   14 22 22 7 18 13 20.   9 22
14 22 14 25 22 9,   26 21 7 22 9   2 12 6
11 26 24 16   7 19 22 8 22   18 7 22 14 8
23 22   8 7 9 12 2   7 19 18 8 14 22 8 8 26 20 22.
7 19 22   15 26 8 7   11 22 9 8 12 13
4 22   4 26 13 7   7 12   16 13 12 4
26 25 12 6 7   12 6 9   24 15 6 25   19 12 6 8 22

18 8   12 6 9   13 12 8 22   2   15 18 7 7 15 22   8 18 8 7 22 9
14 18 8 8   2   20 13 13.

11 22   26 24 22,
16 4 26 14 22

I. 8 19 26 10 6 26 13:
18 11 12 23

II. 24 22 15 15 11 19 12 13 22

III. 21 15 26 8 19 15 18 20 19 7

IV. 25 26 7 7 22 9   2   24 19 26 9 20 22

V. 7 12 12 15 25 12 3

VI. 14 18 24 9 12 4   26 5 22

VII. 25 26 8 16 22 7 25 26 15 15

I. 16 4 26 14 22:
11 12 9 7 26 25 15 22   7 22 15 22 5 18 8 18 12 13

II. 5 18 20 22 12   20 26 14 22 8

III. 21 12 12 7 25 26 15 15

IV. 25 12 7 7 15 22   23   4 26 7 22 9

V. 19 26 13 23   8 26 13 23 7 18 1 22 9

VI. 8   13 26 24 16   11 26 24 16 8

VII. 11 26 11 22 9   7 12 4 22 15 8

First, I wrote out the alphabet from A to Z. Then, I numbered each letter. A=1, B=2, C=3 and so on, until I got to Z=26. I tested my idea with the first few numbers to see if it would translate into a word. 24 15 6 25, became XOFY. That was not a word. My heart sank. I scanned the whole letter again. This time I decided to reverse the alphabet and number the letters from Z to A. Z=1, Y=2, X=3, and so on to A=26, to see if my luck changed.

This time 24 15 6 25 became letters that spelled CLUB. I felt hyped! I wanted to make sure this was not a fluke. So, I tried a few more numbers, 19 12 6 8 22. The numbers spelled out the word HOUSE. It read "CLUBHOUSE". I kept going and the next set of numbers spelled "CHECKLIST". I did it! I had broken the code. I jumped up and down and hugged Saidi. It was time to get ready for school the next day and for bed. I put the Mystery Letter back in my desk drawer, along with my other decoding paperwork. I pulled out my journal.

The case of "Eyes and Ears on Grown-Ups in Action"

April 3rd

Grown-ups fear things kids would never imagine in a million years. My mom was afraid to be my mom. It is hard for me to imagine that. I have only known her as my mom. That is what she's been to me my whole life.

Yaro &

The next day at school, I went looking for Missy Ann. There she was, with her girls, just as I wanted. I stepped up to her with the authority, style, and confidence of a super sleuth. Of course, I had my boys with me. When I was a few feet from her, I called her out in my loud, confident voice, "Missy Ann!"

A bit startled, with a questioning look in her eyes, she gave me a half-smile and said, "Yeah?"

Then I said, "Well, everybody knows you don't call me 'Sherlock' for nothing! I broke the code."

Excited and delighted, Missy Ann started talking real fast as she blurted out "Where is the Mystery Letter? What does it say? Is there something in it that is real private? Do we need to meet after school and talk?"

I said, "Girl, slow down and breathe." I didn't plan to tell her too much at once. I continued, "I am working on the letter tonight and tomorrow. In three days … "

"Three days!" mocked Missy Ann.

I was not going to let her get the upper hand again. I said, "Do you want your letter back? `Cause I can give it back to you today!"

Looking at her lack of options, Missy Ann answered back humbly, "No, I can wait three days."

I reassured her by saying, "I will return the letter to you completely translated. Then, you will know everything."

Missy Ann's eyes lit up as she said, "Okay!"

Everyone knows she likes to know everything, especially other people's business.

Before I walked away, I looked in her eyes and said, "I hope you can handle the facts once I deliver them." I turned and walked away in a veil of mystery, suspense and anticipation.

"What does that mean?" Missy Ann asked.

Her girlfriends wondered aloud, "What is he talking about?"

As he followed behind me, my boy Jamal answered, "You'll find out soon enough!"

After school, my boys and I went over to Magic's Community Center, where my uncle volunteers as a coach when he's home and during the off season. He plays pro-basketball for the L.A. Lakers. We had a snack, did our homework, warmed up shooting hoops, then played basketball.

After the game, Auntie came to pick up Uncle and me. "Yaro," she said, "I am not cooking tonight. Your uncle is treating us to dinner."

Uncle looked questionably at her and asked, "I am?"
Auntie replied, "Are you cooking tonight?"
My uncle said, "Name the restaurant!"

Later, at dinner Auntie told us she was the fund-raising chairwoman for the community center. "We are doing two fund-raisers this year, one for the adults, and a carnival for the kids. Yaro, would you and some of your friends like to help the committee plan the carnival activities?" she asked.

"Sure!" I replied.
"Great! Since it's a fund-raiser for the kids, I think we should let you all help."
"Auntie, I like the way you think!"

When I got home, I took out the garbage and fed Saidi. I don't know if he was so excited because I had finally come home, or because I was feeding him. It didn't really matter though; I was just glad to see Saidi.

I went into the family room and told my parents that Auntie had asked if my friends and I would help her committee plan the carnival. My parents said it was nice of her to include us.

My dad said that since I had been doing my chores and homework without being reminded, he and Mom would take me to World Adventures Amusement Park.

"When?" I blurted out.

My mom said, "Friday after school. We asked your grandparents to babysit so we can go."

"I love the amusement park! I am so excited; I can hardly wait!" I gave both my parents a bear hug before going to my room.

I sat at my desk and took the Mystery Letter from the drawer, along with my decoding materials. Now that the code was broken, decoding the Mystery Letter was a snap! As I continued unveiling the secrets of the Mystery Letter, it looked like Kwame and Shaquan had a clubhouse that they were fully stocking. This clubhouse was a first class set-up, all the way. I laughed out loud as I thought: *Missy Ann is going to lose her mind when she finds out everything they have done, right under her nosey little nose.*

It was almost time to get ready for bed, but I still had to work on my other case. I put the letter away and vowed to finish it tomorrow. Then I pulled out my journal.

The case of "Eyes and Ears on Grown-Ups in Action"

April 4th

There are a lot of grown-ups in kids' lives: our parents, teachers, coaches, relatives, etc. Sometimes it is hard, trying to please all of them, knowing if we don't, there will be consequences! Somehow, that does not seem fair. But, after having dinner with my uncle and auntie tonight, and after talking with my parents, I realized that grown-ups try to please children too.

Yaro &

The next day at school, my teacher, Miss Prim, taught us a lesson on career exploration. We brainstormed career choices. Then we talked about the natural talents, skills, and education we would need to prepare for each profession.

Career Options

Your Natural Talents/Abilities/Interests   Career Options

Dr. Howard Gardner's Multiple Intelligences

Visual/Spatial Intelligence
Can think and create in mental images and pictures.

Visual Arts, Architect, Pilot

Verbal/Linguistic Intelligence
Communicates well through verbal and written expression.

Lawyer

Logical/Mathematical Intelligence
Great with numerical computations, can solve complex problems, detect patterns and utilize scientific information.

Scientist

Bodily/Kinesthetic Intelligence
Hand and eye coordination enjoys physical activity.

Pro Athlete, Chef, Sculptor

Musical/Rhythmic Intelligence
Composing, singing, rhyming,

Singer, Rapper

Miss Prim passed out letters for us to give to our parents, scheduling them to come speak to our class about their careers.

MARTIN LUTHER KING ACADEMY
2020 Martin Luther King Boulevard
Los Angeles, CA 90016

Our Students Success is: **CLEAR**
Career, **L**eadership, **E**ducation, **A**chievement and **R**igor

April 5

Dear Parent,

April is the month we celebrate "Bring Your Child to Work Day." Congratulations if you plan on sharing this experience with your child later on this month. In an effort to expose students to as many professions as possible, we are asking parents to come and talk about their professions with your child's class. To schedule a day and time, please list three possible, dates and times below. I will notify you by e-mail when we have you scheduled. Your child is also writing you a personal invitation to participate that will accompany this letter.

For those parents who are unable to visit the class, any information that you would like to send for me or your child to share with the class is an option. Every job is a valuable and important contribution to society. Any connection you can make regarding the subjects in school that helped you the most in your current position would be great to share with the students.

Parent Name _____ Student Name _____ Phone _____

E-mail Address _____

Dates/Times: First Choice _____ Second Choice _____

Third Choice _____

If you have any questions please feel free to contact me by telephone at (111) 112-0000 or by e-mail: MissPrim@MLKA.edu.

Sincerely,

Miss Prim

Miss Prim
Classroom Teacher

Educating Diverse Learners to Meet the Global Needs of Our World Today and Tomorrow

She also assigned us to write personal persuasive invitations to our parents.

April 5

Dear Dad,

Thank you for taking me to your job every year on "Bring Your Child to Work Day." I always have so much fun at your office. My vocabulary increases when I spend the day observing you and talking to your assistant and secretary. I document my experience every year and report it back to my class.

Could you please come to my school and talk to my class about what you do at your job as a corporate attorney? I know you are very busy. But if you could come, it would mean a lot to me and my classmates.

Love,

Your Son Yaro

P.S. If you do this, some kids might want to become a corporate attorney when they grow up.

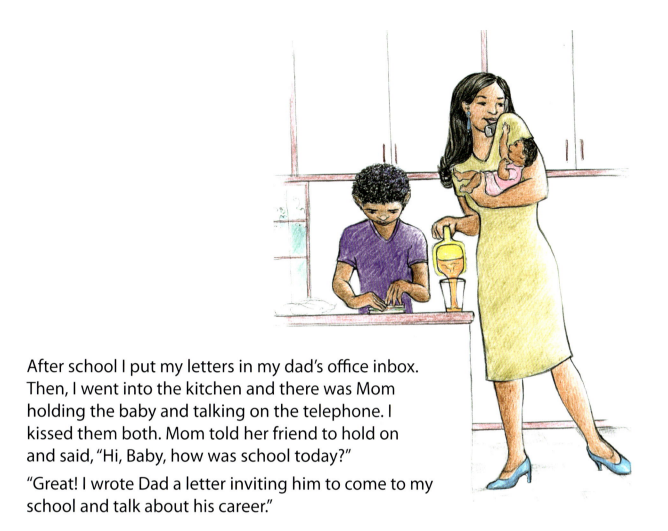

After school I put my letters in my dad's office inbox. Then, I went into the kitchen and there was Mom holding the baby and talking on the telephone. I kissed them both. Mom told her friend to hold on and said, "Hi, Baby, how was school today?"

"Great! I wrote Dad a letter inviting him to come to my school and talk about his career."

"Sounds good honey, but where is this letter?" she asked.
"I put it in Dad's inbox in his office."

"Good!" she said. "That is where I put all of Dad's important mail. He checks his inbox everyday. Do you have any homework today?"

"No, not today, but I am busy working on my own pet project."

Saidi heard my voice and began barking from the backyard. As I washed my hands, Mom said I could have a smoothie, and a slice of turkey and cheese. I rolled the cheese up in the turkey. I asked my mom if she would make me a strawberry and banana smoothie. She did.

After I had my snack, I went into the backyard to feed Saidi. While he was eating, I scooped up his business, if you know what I mean. That is the only part I do not like about having a dog. Saidi followed me back into the house.

In my room, I got busy decoding the Mystery Letter while Saidi lay on the floor chewing his bone. Knowing the code, the Mystery Letter was rapidly revealing its secrets right before my eyes. There was a clubhouse, secret meetings, and destroying evidence. I had to laugh. "The Mouth" needed me to get the goods on her brothers. Imagine that! Somehow, helping Missy Ann didn't seem right. But, I had a lot at stake, so I had to follow through. I leaped to my feet and broke out in song and dance, "Lift, pop your collar, and holla! I got skills!"

With all the excitement, Saidi jumped to his feet, looked at me and started barking! During the commotion, Mom called me to dinner. Saidi has to go outside when we eat.

```
Club House checklist
Shaquan bring the
list of items under
your name. meet us
at the clubhouse the
same day and time
we discussed at our
last meeting. Re
member, after you
pack these items
destroy this message.
```

So, I let him out the back door and washed my hands. At dinner dad said, "I read your letter, Son, and the letter from your teacher. I e-mailed Miss Prim and arranged with her to come to your school tomorrow at 2:30 pm."

"Thanks, Dad!"

He continued, "After I speak to your class, I'll take you home. We'll pick up Mom and head straight to World Adventures Amusement Park."

"Great, Dad. I can't wait!"

The case of "Eyes and Ears on Grown-Ups in Action"

April 5th

Dad works hard all day at his job. Then, he comes home and works most of the evening in his office. If I was a grown-up, I would spend a lot more time after work having fun!

Yaro &

The next morning my boys, Jamal, Carlos, Wen and Ian came by to pick me up for school. As soon as we stepped outside Jamal said, "Yaro, did you get the job done?"

"You know it! Holla! Holla! Your boy's got skills!"

All my boys said, "Yaro's got skills!"

At school, I stayed out of sight during 1st and 2nd recess. I read stories to the kindergarten class. I wanted to build Missy Ann's suspense. At last recess Missy Ann and her girlfriends were on a mission to find me, and they did.

With a smirk on her face and a bite in her voice, Missy Ann spoke, "Have you been hiding from me all day, Yaro?"

With the confidence and the cool of a super sleuth, I said, "No, not at all."

She continued, "This is an 'S' Day for you Yaro. You have two possibilities, an 'S' for success, or an 'S' for shame. Which is it going to be for you? Show me what you got!"

With one smooth move, I pulled the torn, taped, and tattered letter out of my pocket and boldly presented it to Missy Ann. Her eyes were dancing with glee as she received the letter. I had a captivated audience, but all eyes were locked on Missy Ann as she scanned the letter. In a sudden volcanic eruption "The Mouth" screamed, "A clubhouse! Where? When are these meetings, Yaro?"

I looked Missy Ann in the eye, as I asserted myself. "Look, Missy Ann, you asked me to decode the Mystery Letter, and I did. I am not a stalker, and I do not have your brothers under surveillance. That's your job! I'd say this is an 'S Day' for you too, Missy Ann.

"You're slipping!" Jamal piped in. "Oh, no! Say it ain't so, Missy Ann. You're not slipping are you? Say what? Say who? Say you? 'The Mouth' didn't know!"

Missy Ann was shocked and stunned. She just glared at us.

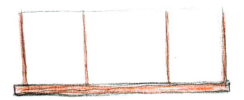

Together, my boys and I did a dance as we sang, "Lift, pop your collar, and holla, holla, Yaro got skills! You heard! Now you know it! Lift, pop your collar, and holla, holla! We all got skills! You heard! Now you know it!" We sang that chorus and danced all the way to the basketball court. I did not stay around for Missy Ann's complete meltdown!

After recess, there was my father in class, waiting. Miss Prim asked me to introduce my guest. I had practiced the introduction with my dad the night before. "This is my dad, Malcolm J. McKnight. He is a corporate attorney and a partner in his law firm, McKnight, Williams, Jackson & Johnson."

Attorneys At Law

Litigation Attorneys for the People

Civil Attorneys: Are used for non-criminal actions. Court proceedings can include divorce, financial disputes, traffic violations and personal injury.

Criminal Law Attorneys: Are used in criminal court proceedings in cases of crimes, petty crimes, and felonies (serious crimes).

Prosecutor Attorneys: Are used by the state or federal government to represent their interests depending on if it is a state or federal crime.

Private Criminal Attorneys: Represent the defendant (the accused). The client pays the attorney.

Public Defender Attorneys: Represent clients who are unable to pay for a private attorney. The state appoints and pays for this attorney.

Corporate Attorneys for Businesses and Corporations

Corporate Attorneys: Represent corporations and businesses. Their focus is on the financial health of the company. They build deals, advises companies on legal rights and obligations.

Corporate Litigation Attorneys: Represent corporations and businesses when things go wrong, a deal goes bad, a Cor_____torney goes to judicial court to represent the company. Dispute resolution, me_____methods used to settle or resolve disputes.

My dad began, "Thank you for that introduction, Son. My firm represents companies that create and develop environmentally friendly products made from organic and natural ingredients. We pride ourselves on 'Corporate Citizenship.' Our purpose is to help companies prosper that promote the healthy state of humans and the planet."

The case of "Eyes and Ears on Grown-Ups in Action"

April 6th

Today was one of the best days of my life. World Adventures Amusement Park was even more fun than I expected! Dad and I like contact rides like bumper cars and roller coasters. We like to raise our hands up in the air, while on the roller coaster, as it coasts, dips and rolls. My dad and I tried to get my mom to go on the "Mammoth Roller Coaster" with us, but she said no. She feels like she gets whiplash after riding on one.

She likes rides that glide through the air like the "Glider" and the "Ferris Wheel." The amusement park was a perfect ending to an "S Day." I had a successful day, and Dad was a hit with my class.

Yaro &

Saturday afternoon, I was outside in my backyard playing with Saidi when Jamal came by. He wanted to know what went down when Missy Ann's brothers found out she was on to them. I told him Kwame and Shaquan had dropped by earlier that day to let me know that we were still cool! They knew Missy Ann's tactics. I said, "Jamal, you won't believe this!"

"What?"
"Everyone in Missy Ann's family, including their cat, has been to the clubhouse." We exploded with laughter!

"So what did her parents say?" asked Jamal. "They said, as far as Missy Ann going to the clubhouse, that is something she will have to work out with her brothers. And so far, man, she's not having any luck!"

Jamal asked, "Yaro, do you think Missy Ann has learned her lesson?"
"Maybe ... "

Suddenly, in the middle of my response, a piercing squeal from a familiar voice. "Yaro! Sherlock, you're not! If you were a real super sleuth, you would know where the clubhouse is!"

Feeling badgered, I said, "Spying on me again, Missy Ann?"

Pretending not to be, she responded, "No! I just happened to be reading this book in my own backyard when I was disturbed by your cackling!"

In a firm voice, I said, "Missy Ann, your case is closed!"

Enraged, Missy Ann threatened, "Yaro, if you do not re-open my case, I am going to tell the whole school you are a 'wannabe sleuth'. You are no super sleuth because a real super sleuth could tell me where the clubhouse is."

I took a deep breath before I responded, "Missy Ann, stop and think! I really don't think you want to remind the whole school how you did not even know what was going on in your own backyard, so to speak. If I recall, you needed me. Jamal, did I deliver?"

Jamal answered, "In black and white, into the hands of someone who didn't know anything! Girl, you need to quit! Now at least you know something! Let me put it another way: Now you know what you don't know!" Jamal and I laughed so hard we cried!

With that Missy Ann stormed off in a huff!

"Jamal, I have to believe there is hope for her. Some people are just slow learners."

Jamal gave me a high five in the air and said, "I'm a witness to that!"

The case of the Mystery Letter

CASE CLOSED!!!

The case of "Eyes and Ears on Grown-Ups in Action."
April 7th

This is my final entry, and then I will closeout this Top Secret Case Study on "Eyes and Ears on Grown-ups in Action." What did I uncover and discover about the grown-ups in my life? They have a lot of responsibilities and pressures. Yes, grown-ups do and say strange things sometimes. Kids may never totally understand them. Sometimes it seems unfair that they have a lot of power over us. Kids are expected to follow their lead, because if we don't there are consequences! But grown-ups do many things to please children too!

Children remind them how to have fun, and that they're still not too old to play! I know that kids are important to grown-ups. My dad says it best: "My children are my main business and my #1 treasure!" Being a grown-up, its no fun!

The case of "Eyes and Ears on Grown-ups in Action"

Yaro &   CASE CLOSED!!!   THE END

TEACHING TOOL

Interactive Educational Appendix for Children, Parents, Educators, and Counselors

Appendix A. NAME ORIGINS

Yaro is a male African name from the Hausa language. We know from the story that Yaro means "son." Hausa is an important trade language. Eighty-five percent of the people living in Niger, Africa speak Hausa.

Saidi is a male African name from the Swahili language. Swahili is a coastal language spoken mainly in Kenya and Tanzania. We know from the story that Saidi means "helper."

Did you know there is power in a name? People are given, or choose, a name for many different reasons. Your name is a part of your identity. Research the origin of your name. Were you named after someone? Did one or both of your parents name you? Did someone else name you? Why was your name chosen for you? Does your name have a meaning like "Yaro" and "Saidi?" These are questions you can discuss with your family.

Appendix B. SELF-DISCOVERY

Self-Determination: "The difference between the impossible and the possible lies in a man's determination." Tommy Lasorda, Major League Pitcher and Manager

We know from the story that Yaro knows he wants to be a detective when he grows up. He's practicing problem solving techniques. These are very useful skills that will help him succeed in his career as a detective. Making observations, documenting information, and having a sense of wanting to do the right thing are all valuable skills. It's never too early to start working toward your career goal(s). If you decide upon a career that you are interested in, start taking steps to develop the skills that will help you be successful.

Self-Awareness: "The man who has no imagination has no wings." Muhammad Ali, World Heavyweight Boxing Champion

Part of self-awareness is to know your strengths, your talents, and discovery of new areas of interest. Do you know it is important to study yourself throughout your life? Question yourself. What is my impression of myself? How would I describe myself to others? Do I feel good about the person I am? What comes naturally and easy to me? What do I believe I would be good at? Am I a good runner, singer, rapper, dancer, or actor? Am I good with math? Am I creative? Do I enjoy arts and crafts? Do I enjoy cooking? Do I enjoy exploring wildlife in their natural habitat? Do I love athletics? Do I like taking things apart and putting them back together? Do I enjoy working with computers or technology? Do I like taking care of sick people, or animals? Do I have any hobbies? Can you imagine a career opportunity in the things that you enjoy doing?

Am I Really Smart? "What a relief it was to discover that I wasn't an idiot! I simply had a learning disability." John H. Johnson - Publisher of Ebony and Jet Magazines

Dr. Howard Gardner studies people, how they think, and how they blend various types of intelligences into their lives. He believes that there are many ways of being smart, and illustrates this in the following chart, called "Multiple Intelligences." Gardner identifies eight intelligences.

Every normal human being has natural gifts, talents, and abilities and uses the eight multiple intelligences. The way in which people use their intelligences makes them an individual and unique. Personal style, and skill level, also contributes to an individual's unique make-up.

The extent to which you develop your multiple intelligences sets you apart from others. Research shows that all forms of intelligence increase as you work toward learning more about any particular subject, or area of interest. So intelligence is something that you can increase.

What's My Talent? "Everybody has talent; it's just a matter of moving around until you've discovered what it is." George Lucas – Academy Award winning Film Maker

Review the Career Exploration chart; on a separate sheet of paper list the eight multiple intelligences. Rate your level of interest on a scale of 1 to 10, 1 being low interest, 10 being high interest. Now, look at the intelligences that you scored highly. Can you think of a career(s) in this area that you would like to explore? What skills would you have to develop to be successful in your career(s) choice(s)? Match the subjects in school you believe would help you in your choice of career(s). Add other professions to the Career Exploration chart. Remember, many people have multiple careers over their lifetime.

Appendix C. DR. HOWARD GARDNER'S MULTIPLE INTELLIGENCES

Your Natural Talents/Abilities/Interests	Career Options
Dr. Howard Gardner's Multiple Intelligences	
Visual/Spatial Intelligence — Can think and create in mental images and pictures.	Visual Arts, Architect, Pilot
Verbal/Linguistic Intelligence — Communicates well through verbal and written expression.	Speaker, Author, Lawyer
Logical/Mathematical Intelligence — Great with numerical computations, can solve complex problems, detect patterns and utilize scientific information.	Computer Programmer, Engineer, Scientist
Bodily/Kinesthetic Intelligence — Good hand and eye coordination enjoys physical activity.	Professional Athlete, Chef, Sculptor
Musical/Rhythmic Intelligence — Enjoys composing, singing, rhyming, rapping, or playing a musical instrument.	Singer, Musician, Rapper
Interpersonal Intelligence - Has the ability to relate well to a variety of people.	Mediator, Counselor, Police Officer
Intrapersonal Intelligence — Self- study. Understanding your feelings, motivations, and knowing how your actions affect your world.	Philosopher, Clergy, Psychologist
Naturalist Intelligence — Has the ability to relate to and connect with nature, plant life, or animals. May be able to identify a variety of rocks and fossils.	Agriculturalist, Archeologist, Paleontologist

Appendix D. GOAL SETTING

Potential: "Others will underestimate us, for although we judge ourselves by what we feel capable of doing, others judge us only by what we have already done."
Henry Wadsworth Longfellow – American Poet

Suppose you want to be a doctor, but you know that you struggle in math and science. Your motivation is high but, so far you have not made the grades required to become a doctor. Does this mean you should give up on that career choice? No, it means if you truly want to be a doctor, then you have to make a plan to accomplish your goal. Preparation and hard work are the keys to achieving a goal.

Goal Setting Steps:

1) Begin with an Idea/Dream/Goal.
2) Become confident that you can achieve your goal.
3) Map out a plan of action, set timelines and completion dates for successful steps.
4) Write an affirmation, slogan, chant or motto as encouragement to achieve your goal.
5) Identify people who can support you in your goal and let them know how.
6) Implement your plan.
7) Evaluate your progress.
8) If changes are necessary for success, make them and re-evaluate your progress.

Appendix E. THE BLUEPRINT

Preparation: "Education is the most powerful weapon which you can use to change the world."
Nelson Mandela – President of South Africa 1994-1999

Example of the Goal Setting Process:

Goal: I want to be a doctor.

Confidence: I know I am capable of achieving my goal of being a doctor.

Plan: I struggle in math and science; I will get extra tutoring in those areas.

Timeline and Steps: Today, I will sign up for after school tutoring. I will attend tutoring everyday after school. Science is difficult for me but, easier than math. So, three days a week I will focus on tutoring in math, and the other two days I will concentrate on science. In two weeks I will take a test in both math and science to determine my progress.

Motto: "I know I have what it takes to do my best in math and science. Put me to the test; I'll do my best."

Support: I spoke with my parents about my math and science goals. They will quiz me and work with me at home. My math and science teachers are proud of my take charge attitude, and are willing to tutor me after school.

Action: I have been working on my plan, attended after school tutoring on a daily basis and received additional help from my teachers. My parents have taken turns quizzing me at home.

Evaluate: The extra support I have received from my parents and teachers, has helped to improve my understanding of math and science. My tests scores have gone up and I feel great about my accomplishments.

Appendix F. CHARACTER: WHO YOU REALLY ARE

Building Character: "Be more concerned with your character than with your reputation. Your character is what you really are while your reputation is merely what others think you are." John Wooden – Member of the Basketball Hall of Fame as a player and coach

What is character? Character is what you are made of, your inner ingredients. Who you really are, your character, is reflected in your outward actions. The thoughts and feelings we hold in our hearts and minds shine through in our behavior and actions. Character traits are developed and learned over time. What are character traits? We have a mixture of both positive and negative character traits. Examples of positive character traits are caring, honesty, trustworthiness, responsibility, dependability, respectfulness, thoughtfulness, generosity, fairness, forgiveness, and understanding. Examples of negative character traits are self-centeredness, disrespect, unreliability, being unforgiving, deceitfulness, selfishness, insensitivity, being judgmental, and jealous.

"Successful people succeed because they learn from their failures."
Bettina Flores - Author

Why is it important to cultivate as many positive character traits as possible? Character traits guide your life. For every action or choice you make, there is a reaction or a consequence. It is more likely that your consequences of making positive choices will bring you a sense of satisfaction or happiness. We all make poor choices sometimes. This can be a good learning experience because it can help us to grow and learn from our mistakes. At times, seeing the results of negative choices we have made makes a lasting impression on us, and enables us to make better choices in the future. However, if you repeatedly make poor choices and it appears that you are not learning from those choices, it could result in people perceiving you as having bad character. Bad character leads people to believe that they cannot trust you. As a result, your options and choices will be limited and you may feel undervalued and like an outcast.

"A man who stands for nothing will fall for anything."
Malcolm X – Minister and Social Activist Leader

What does character have to do with a career? Certain professions have a code of conduct. As a member of that profession you must take an oath or agree to follow a set of moral and ethical standards. This is true in many professions in which the public has to entrust their well-being or their lives to professionals such as doctors, lawyers, therapists, and police officers. All of them take an oath or agree to conduct themselves in a manner that is aligned with the positive character traits expected of a professional in that field.

"It is not your environment, it is not your history, it is not your education or ability; it is the quality of your mind that predicts your future."
Dr. Benjamin Mays – President of Morehouse College 1940-1967

The Honorable Judge Greg Mathis of the Judge Mathis Television Show was a bright and very observant teenager, raised in a loving, strict, and religious home. He chose to rebel and stray away from some of the positive teachings that his mother had nurtured in their home. He was attracted to the seemingly successful lifestyle of the "street hustlers"; the fast money, nice cars, and fashionable clothes. As a teen, he developed a reputation among some in authority as a person exhibiting poor character. Greg was in the court system when a judge offered him two choices: either go to school and get a G.E.D., or go to jail. You might think that this was an easy decision.

Who would choose jail? Some people might choose jail if they were seeking "street credibility." This would reflect twisted thoughts and distorted thinking. This is why it is important to be a critical thinker and look at the consequences of your actions now and how it can affect your future choices. A criminal record in your youth could potentially limit your future career choices.

Greg decided to use his brilliant mind in a way that would benefit him and others in positive ways. We always have choices. It is your ability to make quality decisions that will lead you to either help society or take away from it. Now, the Honorable Judge Greg Mathis is a living example of how you can change your life. If you have the vision, believe in yourself, cultivate positive character, and do the work.

Appendix G. THE POWER OF FAITH AND BELIEF

"Faith is taking the first step even when you don't see the whole staircase."
Dr. Martin Luther King, Jr. – Minister and Civil Rights Leader

Dr. Martin Luther King, Jr. not only had a dream, but he had a plan for implementing his dream. He was a leader in nation building. He motivated people and uplifted their hopes and dreams. Dr. King fought for justice where there was injustice. He had a vision for all humans to live together in peace and harmony regardless of religion, race, color, nationality, or creed.

Dr. Martin Luther King, Jr. endured great adversity during his life. He was spit upon, verbally abused, and physically attacked; yet through it all he remained steadfast to his convictions of non-violence. Dr. King said it best: "The ultimate measure of a man is not where he stands in moments of comfort and convenience, but where he stands at times of challenge and controversy." As a minister and through his faith in God, Dr. Martin Luther King, Jr. was able to overcome great adversity. He is an American Hero who rose to the world stage as a recipient of the Noble Peace Prize in 1964. His heroic life made a difference, and he left the world his legacy.

To make anything significant in your life happen you have to have a dream, a goal, a vision, and a plan. Then, you have to have faith, belief, determination, and be willing to do the hard work to see it through. Finally, you must have the opportunity. This is the blueprint to success.

"I look to a day when people will not be judged by the color of their skin, but by the content of their character."
Dr. Martin Luther King, Jr.

Appendix H. MAKING IT HAPPEN IN YOUR SCHOOL

Bring the World of Work Into Your School

Yaro's class at Martin Luther King Academy bridged the gap between education and the world of work by inviting parents into their classroom to share information about their careers.

Here are some ways you can celebrate the world of work as a whole school. Invite the local Junior Achievement organization into your school. Through their school program students engage in hands on activities, enacting duties of officials in society, managing commerce for the good of the community, as they strengthen their understanding of the world of work.

Send out an open invitation to the parents of the entire student body. Ask who would be willing to speak about their career in the classroom(s) or at a school wide assembly. Ask who would host students at their job site so they can see in person what working for a particular company or organization is like.

Additional things you can do to provide meaningful and relevant connections to places of business: Seek out companies that provide job shadowing, mentorship, and internship opportunities for high school and college students. These work experiences are a good way to get first hand experience working in the real world in your field of interest.

Career Awareness Exploration

Web sites for kids, teens, parents, and educators to get started:

http://www.ja.org

http://www.jabizkids.com

http://www.kidsnewsroom.org

http://www.youngbiz.com

http://www.acrnetwork.org

http://www.daughtersandsonstowork.org

Appendix I. PARENTS' ROLE

"Parenting is the greatest performance of your life. Your home is your theater, the script improvisational, and your children are your captive audience."
Helen L. Edwards – Author, Counselor, Educator, and Actress

Parents must lay the foundation for their children's life journey toward success. Parents must recognize the talents, skills, abilities, and gifts in their children and point them out to them. If you believe in them and their abilities, then they will believe in themselves. Your children watch how you live your life. If your words match your actions, then that is a powerful message to your children. If they see you reading, eating healthy, and being physically active, then they are more likely to acquire those same habits. Exposure to books, athletics, and social organizations like scouts, boys and girls' clubs, and cultivating spirituality is crucial, whether through traditional or home taught methods. Trips to museums, zoos, aquariums, and active involvement in your child's education will give your child a fighting chance in today's global world and in the 21st century.

"Parents who push their children to achieve and fortify them with love can withstand whatever the larger society might throw at them." - President Barack Hussein Obama-First African American to accept the Democratic Party Nomination for President of the United States of America. On November 4, 2008 America elected Barack Obama as the Nation's First Black African American President.

Fostering these parenting techniques lays the foundation for children to withstand challenges and persevere onto greatness by achieving their goals and dreams.

About The Author

Helen L. Edwards has been an elementary school counselor for over a decade. She is president of the Washington Association of Multicultural Counseling and Development (WAMCD) which is a division of the Washington Counseling Association (WCA) and a member of the American School Counselor Association (ASCA). In addition Ms. Edwards is a Cross-Cultural Competency Trainer for the Washington Education Association (WEA). The focus of her trainings and workshops is to facilitate ways to effectively promote cross-cultural communication and understanding of diversity for educators, administrators, and human resource personnel.

As an author it is essential to Ms. Edwards that all children see themselves reflected in her books. She enjoys writing children's stories that are relevant, entertaining, educational, interactive, and empowering to children. Add her first book Clara's Imagination to your child's literary collection.

About The Illustrator

Chi Lam Chan was born in Hong Kong. When he was seven and a half years old, he and his family moved to Staten Island, New York. He attended the School of Visual Arts and Fashion Institute of Technology before moving to Seattle, Washington, where he completed his FBA in Illustration at Cornish College of the Arts.

About The Colorist

Al Doggett is an award-winning illustrator and a native of New York. He is a graduate of Fashion Institute of Technology (FIT) in New York City. Al currently resides in Seattle, Washington, where he runs a full service art studio. He conducts workshops and gives presentations to children at schools in the community. Children are an integral part of his life and are depicted in many of his works.

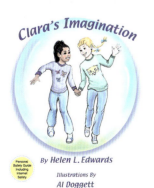

Al Doggett is the illustrator of Helen L. Edwards first book Clara's Imagination. In addition, Al is also the colorist and did the cover design for Yaro the Super Sleuth in the Case of the Mystery Letter.

ISBN 13 978-0-9765414-0-0
ISBN 10 0-9765414-0-8